Ethnicity

The Inclusive Church Resource

DARTON · LONGMAN + TODD

First published in Great Britain in 2015 by
Darton, Longman and Todd Ltd
1 Spencer Court
140 – 142 Wandsworth High Street
London SW18 4JJ

ISBN 978-0-232-53070-4

A catalogue record for this book is available from the
British Library

Phototypeset by Judy Linard
Printed and bound by Imak Ofset, Turkey

Contents

Acknowledgements

Inclusive Church is grateful to all who have made this book possible.

In particular we would like to acknowledge the enthusiasm and support for this book from David Moloney at Darton Longman and Todd. We would also like to acknowledge our thanks to Allison Ward for her work in compiling the indexes for the Inclusive Church Resource Book series

We are grateful to the Churches Equality Practitioner Group for ideas and suggestions for this book series.

The Inclusive Church Resource Book series has only been made possible through the generosity of those who have contributed time, stories, reflections and resources for these books. Thank you to each contributor.

It is our hope that all that is shared here will encourage others to go further in the work of creating a more inclusive and welcoming church.

About Inclusive Church

Inclusive Church was formed in 2003. From the start, churches and individuals have signed up to the statement of belief as a way of indicating their desire to see a more accepting and open church.

The Inclusive Church
'Statement of Belief'

We believe in inclusive church – church which does not discriminate, on any level, on grounds of economic power, gender, mental health, physical ability, race or sexuality. We believe in church which welcomes and serves all people in the name of Jesus Christ; which is scripturally faithful; which seeks to proclaim the Gospel afresh for each generation; and which, in the power of the Holy Spirit, allows all people to grasp how wide and long and high and deep is the love of Jesus Christ.

www.inclusive-church.org

Introduction

Rosemarie Mallett is a Barbadian-British inner city parish priest in London. She started out as an academic historian of the Caribbean, Africa and Black Britain, first working in Africa and the Caribbean. She returned to the UK to pursue a doctorate in sociology and started work as a senior research sociologist, with a focus on ethnicity and mental health. Through community activism and church engagement she moved from academia to become a parish priest. She is presently a member of General Synod in the Church of England, and has served on two national Synod committees on gender and ethnic inclusion. She is also currently the national chair of Affirming Catholicism and a Trustee of Inclusive Church.

Unity and diversity:
A Theology of Ethnicity

I was forced to start thinking about the connections between ethnicity and faith when I was seven. That was the age I migrated to the United Kingdom as a confident, cheeky Caribbean Anglican. I came from Barbados as a British subject to join family members, but I quickly learnt that I was not considered Barbadian or British in my new home, but instead had to accept a new and designated identity as a 'coloured' West Indian (those were the politest of the names I was called in my new home). I also found that I and my family were not welcomed in the local Anglican Church, and although I was enrolled in the nearest Church of England primary, the family attended the local Methodist church. Within a few months of arrival, I had had to reconfigure my understanding of who I was and how I was to live out my faith so as to fit into my new context. Thus before I could even articulate what they meant, faith and ethnicity became major constructs in my life. What I did know was that I felt excluded from the majority community around me due to skin colour and ethnicity, and that these two aspects of my identity also excluded me from the church family that I had been born into. I certainly had no theology of ethnicity to guide me, and no sense of the inclusive love of the Godhead.

Long before my arrival in the UK in the late 1960s, secular society had been grappling with issues of race and ethnicity, culture and cultural integration as a result of increasing heterogeneity in its population. Every wave of migration of ethnically/visibly/religiously different people has opened up a discourse on identity and difference and the impact of multiculturalism. As Jagessar states, the changing national and global landscape has motivated the majority ethnic groups in European nations to question their own sense of ethnicity and identity. For example, every school in the UK must now teach their students the essential elements of Britishness.[1] Indeed, there are few academic institutions in Europe where issues of ethnic identity are not researched and debated. Large scale migration of people of colour has also accentuated difference and exacerbated levels of racial intolerance and flagrant racism. There are few European countries that have not enacted legislation to deal with issues of racism and inequality.

Why does this matter to the church of God, the space and place where the highest unity of all people has been achieved through the salvific love of Jesus Christ? The church, like all other institutions is made up of people drawn from all the nations of the world. The large scale migration of Christian people of colour to the UK after the 1950s, opened up the discourse on faith and ethnicity identity,

[1] Secretary of State for Justice and Lord Chancelor (2007), *The Governance of Britain* (CM7170) Crown Copyright

on the inclusive nature of the God, and the role of the church in reflecting ethnic diversity. While many Christians would espouse the notion that 'we are all one in Christ', a great many Christian Caribbean migrants found themselves excluded from the mainstream church, which contributed to the establishment and growth of ethno-specific churches since the 1960s. It is a fact that these churches now have the fastest growing church congregations[2] in many European nations and the UK.[3] This is not to understate the numerical growth of Black and Minority Ethnic members of the mainstream churches since the nadir of the 1950s and 60s.[4] However, in most cases the overarching trope of unity in Christ has worked to deny the impact of ethnic diversity and difference in those churches, and has denied the opportunity for people of minority ethnic groups (in particular visibly different groups) bringing all of who they are in the service of Christ. While people of colour now feel much

[2] David Goodhew (Ed) (2012) *Church Growth in Britain, 1980 to the Present, Cranmer Hall, UK, Ashgate Contemporary Ecclesiology*

[3] Andrew Rogers (2013) Being *Built Together A Story of New Black Majority Churches in the London Borough of Southwark: Final Report.* Roehampton University

[4] Peter Brierley *(2011) UK Church Statistics, 2005-2015* Tonbridge: ADBC Publishers

more welcome into mainstream churches, and in parts of the United Kingdom make up the majority of the congregations in some churches, they are barely present at leadership levels. The rise of Black Christian churches throughout Europe, has given lie to the myth that people of colour do not desire or are not ready to accept church leadership. However, mainstream churches have been reluctant or unwilling to engage in honest dialogue on the issues that stem from ethnic diversity and such discourse is seen at best as a challenge and at worse as an accusation of racism. This leaves little or no place to discuss racial justice and racial reconciliation at individual and institutional level. In general the debate on ethnicity and the mainstream church has centred around inclusion, on counting people in. In many cases such inclusion has been focused on people of colour joining in and trying not to be seen to be different to the majority. However, inclusion works best when everyone can most be themselves. Inclusion should not diminish difference but rather celebrate it. The affirmation of ethnic diversity can give the individual believer and the local congregation a unifying sense of social cohesion and belonging, through better understanding of self and others.

All theology is, of course, contextual, and specific, as it seeks to understand and explicate the presence of God in the lives of people of faith and of the church. A theology of ethnicity offers the church a way forward. It gives the church permission to embrace the concept that diversity is an intrinsic God-value for the life and witness of the church. Getting the right balance between unity and diversity will always be difficult, but acknowledgement, acceptance and inclusion of difference allows the church to be an intentional community of radical welcome and engagement, living out the gospel commandment to love God, and our neighbours as ourselves[5]. The contributions in this collection demonstrate the ways in which God's kingdom values of unity and diversity are interwoven throughout the word and the world.

---

[5] Estaban Lugo (2013) A Theology of Ethnic Diversity: God's Mosaic. *Christian Educators Journal.*

PART 1
Experience

*Stories from lived experience are central
to this book. It would be easy to skip
this section and read the theological
reflection or look at the resources. The
stories here are real and speak of different
people's experience; they help us begin to
understand something of the complexity
of issues that are involved when we
begin to think about issues related
to ethnicity.*

*We are grateful to these story-tellers for
their honesty. Our theological reflection
and practical outworking should
follow from these accounts of lived
experience, so please take time
to read these stories carefully.*

Chine's story

Chine Mbubaegbu is director of communications at the Evangelical Alliance and the author of Am I Beautiful?, *which explores body image, race and faith. She studied theology and religious studies at Cambridge University and is a trustee of the Bible Society, the Christian Enquiry Agency, the Church & Media Network and the Sophia Network.*

I stood one of 20,000 others, my arms stretched high over my head, my heart pounding with each chord of the bass; my ears tuned in to the harmonies of the passionate gospel vocals. I had made my return to the Festival of Life, an annual event put on by the Pentecostal denomination the Redeemed Christian Church of God at the ExCel centre in London. It felt familiar. I had often attended the all-night 'holy ghost event' as a child. I remember looking forward to it. I remember struggling to keep my eyes open as the fervent prayers continued into the early hours of the morning.

17

I remember believing that here was where God is.

Aged 30, I am back in a place which feels so familiar; but with a theology degree from Cambridge under my belt and many, many years spent in churches in the predominantly white home counties; my Christian life now seemed far removed from what it had been growing up. But despite feeling like I had landed in some long-forgotten place; there was something all-too-familiar about being back at the Festival of Life. Something about it felt like home. The music, the familiar names, the harmonies, the animated hand gestures, the styles of prayer. Familiar yet so very alien.

I was born in Lagos, Nigeria, believed to be Africa's most populous city with an estimated population somewhere between 17.5 and 21 million. The city creaks with the weight of humanity; its hustle and bustle like none I've experienced anywhere else. My parents lived there although we are from the Igbo tribe in the south-east of the country. The Igbos are a proud, hard-working people for whom storytelling is the glue that holds communities together. But when I was four years old, in 1988, my parents moved the family, including me and my two younger sisters, from Nigeria to Greenwich, south-east London. Until then I suppose like many other four-year-olds regardless of where they are from I had no concept of my ethnicity, let alone that mine was different to most of those around me in reception class.

I remember the first moment of realisation of what I looked like. I was five years old and our teacher had asked us to draw a self-portrait. So I picked up the pencil and drew an outline of myself. I picked up a blue pencil and coloured in my eyes. I picked up a yellow pencil and lovingly drew my long, straight, blonde locks. I took up a pink pencil and gave myself rosy cheeks. I thought that was what I looked like. Because that's what most of the other little girls in my class looked like. But it wasn't until one of my friends turned to me, took one look at my drawing and said: 'That's not you.' And it dawned on me that it wasn't. I was something 'other'.

As humans we often fear people we perceive as 'the other'. Perhaps it's human nature to stick to your own, to be like everyone else around you, because there is a belief deep down that that's where we will be most comfortable with people just like us.

I had returned to the Festival of Life as part of my role as director of communications at the Evangelical Alliance. In a show of solidarity, members of the Alliance's One

People Commission, a body of key national leaders from across different ethnic minorities brought together to celebrate diversity while promoting unity, had attended the event; as had the Archbishop of Canterbury Justin Welby who gave an address. As I looked around me, I took note of the fact that there were a number of different ethnicities of church leaders represented in what was predominantly a black majority church event. And I was struck by how unusual it was. Because I am so used to seeing monochrome churches. Members of congregations gathered with others who look like them.

It was only when I started working for a para-Church organisation that I realised how deep the separation lines between ethnicities within the Church ran. I became aware of the assumption that if you were a certain colour, you went to a certain type of church. I recall sitting in a meeting about some wider Church issue and someone asking: 'What would the black majority churches think?'

I glanced up and realised that the question had been posed at me. All eyes were on me, waiting for me to respond on behalf of black-Christian-kind. What I do remember is thinking: wow, they're asking me because I'm .... black. They thought that because I am black I must go to a certain type of church. They thought that black Christians go to black majority churches. Which meant that somewhere in their subconscious minds, the Church divided along ethnic lines. I was deeply saddened by this. Not because I am in any way ashamed of my black-ness. I'm proud of my heritage and it's an important part of my identity. But it is not the only thing by which my identity is defined. I'm a woman. I'm an alumna of my university. I'm a Manchester United supporter. I'm a Londoner. I'm a journalist. I'm a Take That lover. I am … not very cool. So I would find it odd going to a Church of Women, a Manchester United Supporters' church, the Church of the Uncool, or the Church of the Latter-Day Take That lovers, for that matter. Heaven forbid. But I was saddened upon realising – shock horror – that it is actually possible to pick and choose your church depending on your ethnicity or your country of origin. You can find Polish churches, Chinese churches, Spanish churches, 'black majority churches'.

I realised the depth of feeling that it evoked in me and the sense that there was something so wrong about it all. Because I think, if we're honest, what often lies at the heart of this type of separation is prejudice, preconceptions about those who we would perceive as 'other'.

I don't remember prejudice listed among the gifts of the spirit.

What is important to note though is that I don't think many leaders of 'ethnic' churches set out to have their pews filled with members from one ethnic background. But humans are humans. Even new community Christians like to stick to their own kind. A church leader from a certain background will be attractive to those from a similar background, while those from a totally different background may choose to worship elsewhere. But I'm not sure that when Christ called us to 'be one' as he does in John 17, that he intended us to worship and fellowship only with those people who look like us, who like what we like, who speak the same language or come from the same place. 'When the day of Pentecost came, they were all together in one place,' we hear in Acts 2. In one place.

As human Christians, we cannot pretend that this is easy. Often with difference of background and culture and identity comes conflict. But conflict is inevitable and important. I realise that for some, ethnic origin is their number one way of identifying themselves. I realise that among the people in our beautifully diverse country, there are those who have moved here and are not yet able to speak English well, who want to worship God in their mother tongue and to fellowship with people in their own language. I also realise how isolated people can feel when they sit in church unable to understand what's going on, unable to communicate with others because of language and cultural barriers.

But I think Jesus calls us to what Owen Hylton in *Crossing the Divide*[6] describes as 'radical inclusiveness'. Nobody said it was easy. I think it's our responsibility as Christian leaders to be proactive in making our churches as diverse as possible.

George Yancey in *One Body, One Spirit* writes: '*A multiracial church is a church in which no one racial group makes up more than 80 per cent of the attendees of at least one of the major worship services.*'[7] I believe that's what we need to aim towards.

For many years, I attended a New Frontiers church and loved it primarily because its congregation came from a variety of different social and cultural backgrounds. It wasn't perfect, but in so many ways it reflected the diversity we're called to. It was a church which stood in a leafy suburb in Kent, but on a

[6] Owen Hylton, *Crossing the Divide, IVP 2009*

[7] George Yancey, *One Body, One Spirit, IVP 2003*

Sunday morning I would see the white British, black British, white Africans, black Africans, Europeans, those from the Middle East and lots more besides. One Sunday I remember we heard prayers in Punjabi. But diversity of course is not just about race. I loved the church because there were newborn babies and 90-year-olds. There were married couples, widows, divorcees and singletons. There were taxi drivers, journalists, investment bankers, teachers, doctors, hairdressers, students, shop assistants, and retired people. There were the able-bodied and the disabled.

There were people with problems. And people who may have been totally different from you in the world's eyes, who held your hand as you walked through those problems. Our society is becoming increasingly multicultural. But a multicultural Church isn't just about political correctness. A multicultural, diverse Church is beautifully symbolic of the God whose very essence is unity.

The Church therefore should be the last place where, before entering, I put on the Cloak of Race and stand side by side with those sporting the same attire as me. The Church should be the one place where the cloak matters least; where we stand together with one sole, unifying identity.

And it's that amazing sense of unity that I felt as I stood once again among the multitude gathered at the Festival of Life. There was for me personally a tangible sense of coming home; of being among many people of my own racial identity. People for whom their ethnicity may have been a vital part of who they are. But I was even more struck as I looked around me and saw people from many different nationalities joined in worship to the God in whom all people and things hold together. I felt hopeful that the future of the Church is not one divided among ethnic lines but one in which the ethnic and social barriers that cause us to live in fellowship only with people like us are broken down. One people, with one hope, gather in 'one place'.

Nikki's story

The Revd Nikki Mann is Assistant Curate at All Saints in Stamford and an Ambassador for Inclusive Church.

It's strange that this has become a different narrative from the one I was going to share, it turns out that what I thought was 'my mum's and our story' was not the story she holds! Nevertheless the painful story of West Indian immigrants looking forward to being part of their 'Mother' Anglican Church and other churches in England but being rejected due to racism is well documented.

In the poignant hymn 'I the Lord of Sea and Sky', it says 'I have heard my people cry' and I wonder if God awakens her people to feel, or at least to try to understand, the pain of past and present rejection and to work against it. My awareness of 'pain' came whilst training to be a Priest and is one of the reasons why being part of 'Inclusive Church' matters so much to me. So as I write this I am called now to reflect on my experience (with inputs from my mum and sisters) of being a mixed parentage (West Indian and British) child.

My mother was 'recruited' (due to employee shortages) to come to England from Barbados to train as a nurse. A very long journey by boat, she left behind her midwife mother, headmaster father, four brothers and wider family and friends to travel here. As these were the days before 'cheap' travel it was possible she might not get to see them again for many years. Sadly her father, my grandfather, died before she was able to return many years later. Despite this wrench she speaks warmly of those nurse training years where they were looked after and protected by the matrons, with strict curfews and tales of having to sneak back in through windows! Friendships were made that have lasted until this day.

It was on a weekend trip to Jaywick in Essex that she met my father. My father grew up in Clacton on Sea, his parents were strong supporters of the (now) Royal British Legion and he decided at an early age he wanted to join the RAF and see the world. He had already been to the Middle East and Africa so that by the time he met my mother that evening he was in effect 'colour blind'. Mum being the life and soul of the party grabbed his attention and they hit it off immediately. They married in Lincoln in 1964.

My grandparents were initially welcoming of mum, but then said that they would not meet her, so she was not invited back to the family home for a while. This remained the case until my eldest sister was born in 1965.

My eldest sister has 'white' coloured skin and as a toddler had blond hair. I asked mum whether people thought she was her nanny. She said it was not that people doubted that she was her mum, more that people were just very surprised that she was white! A few years later they were posted to Singapore, where my middle sister was born, with me following a couple of years later back in Oxford. The two of us have what might be termed 'brown' coloured skin.

I used the term 'mixed parentage' earlier instead of 'mixed race' having been told quite sternly by a Black tutor at University 'Nikki we all belong to one human race'. Who can argue with that?! My sister has also reminded me of how horrid the term 'half-caste' was/is, as if we were not quite fully finished or fully whole. She prefers (as I do now having heard it!) to use the term 'dual heritage', which does appear to say more about cultural background rather than colour mixing, especially as we are all of course a 'mix' of our conceiving parents' genes. I love the bit in the film *Madagascar* where Marty the Zebra is discussing his identity: is he black with white stripes or white with black stripes? Both, neither, does it matter?

My father left the RAF and in the 1970s we moved to Middlesex where he joined British Airways. Having discounted staff travel meant we were now able to see our family in Barbados, which was wonderful. So our holidays were split between the two seaside resorts of Clacton and Barbados!

Our address now being more permanent, mum wanted us to grow up in an Anglican Church. My understanding of our experience was that we were not made welcome due to 'our colour'. My mother felt that it was simply that the priest was generally unwelcoming to all children. My mother has always been confident and well loved. As a nurse all her patients loved her. I remember one calling her 'Chalky' which didn't bother her, but it bothered me. I wonder how many offensive comments were, and still are, written off as just 'unintended or friendly banter'. The current investigations of racist tweets within the football profession have highlighted this.

I remember as a seven-year-old being called

'Chocolate Ice Cream' by the child of a family friend. This struck me as very peculiar and I cogitated for days whether this indeed could be an insult, I knew it was intended as one but as I very much liked both of the components it seemed very odd!

We joined a local Congregational Church where we were very welcomed and were 'family' (mum still is) for many years. Hospitable mum would invite all the youth club children in on the way to or after 'Club'. My elder sister recalls, 'I was bullied at school not because I looked black or from a minority ethnic group, but because the kids in question knew my Mum's skin colour. What used to tee me off most was that they were happy to come to our house on the way to youth club at the church ... accept Mum's hospitality ... and then turn into racist bullies on the way back from school.' My middle sister and I did not experience this.

I asked my elder sister who has very tight curly hair if she and mum (who usually straightened her hair), had chosen to wear their hair as afros for a time as a 'statement' of their ethnicity. This was her reply: 'I didn't know I was gonna end up with an afro. I just wanted to get my hair cut like other kids did!' I did something similar as a teenager wanting a new hairstyle like my friend's but remain fearful of hairdressers to this day after the hairdresser said to me, 'Well, the only thing we can do with your hair is cut it off.' Thankfully I just walked out and am now very content with my unruly mop of curls.

Mostly our experience of being of 'dual heritage' (yes, a much better term!) has been a positive embrace of both cultures and acceptance within the communities in which we have lived; this embrace has continued with 'our children', the next generation. However I know that for many young Black and ethnic minority people this has not been the case and they have experienced intolerable verbal and physical assault and rejection.

Most of my reflections have been about growing up in the 1970s and 1980s, but if we roll forward to 2014 during a Mothers' Prayers Group we sat in tears one evening as one of our mums shared how a seven-year-old boy (the same age as my son is now) had been in tears because children in the playground had told him they were not allowed to play with him anymore because he is Black. I told a fellow Black ordinand friend later and with painful echoes she said 'Get over it, my daughter is abused most days, it's the way it is'. Being insulted because of the colour of your skin, the perfect way God created you, is the way it is?

I was so pleased when Black Theology was to be part of my theological training but was disappointed to learn it was only an 'optional' element that year and as most students had few ethnic faces in their congregations, most questioned, as I initially did, whether it could be 'relevant' to their congregation. The uneasy thought process of 'we don't have that problem because we don't really have any ethnic minorities' grew when I read *Struggle in Babylon* by Kenneth Leech.[8] If it is a problem only when we have ethnic minorities in our congregation, does this not therefore imply that they are 'the problem', and that the issue is 'out there' and therefore not relevant to us? Racism and exclusion is rooted in accepting a status quo that 'doesn't affect me'.

When I sat in a friendly house group to discuss the black theology article I had written, one of the lovely church women said to me, 'I have had a day like a nigger slaving in a log pile'; then, looking at me, said, 'Oh I shouldn't really say that should I?'

---

[8] Kenneth Leech, *Struggle in Babylon: Racism in the Cities and Churches of Britain*, SPCK, 1988.

I have had comments like 'Well you're not really Black anyway are you?' As if it shouldn't then really be of concern to me. I am still unsure of quite how brown or black you need to be in people's eyes to be 'Black'! I have a Black identity of which I am very proud. Interestingly I have never felt the need to say I have a White identity of which I am also very proud, which I am, is that because maybe there is an absorbed internal assumption that White needs no explanation of acceptance to it? Oh to live in God's diverse beautiful creation with no label boundaries at all!

I am very sensitive to negativity surrounding the use of the word 'black'. Maybe you are thinking it's just a colour, but when you are living constantly with black negativity, and white positivity it can subtly reinforce stereotypes; language matters. A colour system in a primary school has 'black' as the really 'naughty' board, imagine you are possibly the only 'black' face in your class, in your school, might this help or hinder the development of a positive self-identity? My new email provider as opposed to using 'trustworthy' and 'untrustworthy' for contacts has 'white list' (for trustworthy) and 'black list' (for untrustworthy). I have felt uncomfortable hearing preaching about the 'blackness' of sins, and how they can be washed 'white' and clean. I think I have heard a speaker say there are something like thirty negative uses of 'black' in our language, compared to only three for 'white'.

Reflecting on my journey and the experiences of the past and present generations of so many has been empowering but also deeply uncomfortable at times. I have been fortunate to see Christ's transformative and reconciling purposes at work, experiencing first hand God's intention of inclusion and representation within his body. Within the same year of my being ordained in the Church, my mother received the British Empire Medal for outstanding services to nursing in her adopted country and my parents celebrated their Golden Wedding anniversary. How very special is a picture of my parents (mum with her medal), me (with my dog collar) and the Bishop of Lincoln outside Lincoln Cathedral (the city they married in) following my ordination, as a celebration of all these special things.

I believe God wants her Church and communities to be as beautiful and diverse as all creation and by acceptance and inclusion they can be.

Mukti's story

Mukti Barton did not know that her colour and ethnicity could be the cause of her oppression until she came from India to Britain in 1975. Now she raises awareness about the effects of the issues of colour and ethnicity on theology and church and empowers people to build an inclusive church. Mukti is the author of Rejection, Resistance and Resurrection: Speaking out on Racism in the Church *(London: DLT, 2005).*

The day I set foot in Britain with my White English husband, Stephen, I was profoundly humiliated at Heathrow Airport by the structure of the country because of my colour and ethnicity. This experience was deeply shocking for an Indian Christian coming to a Christian country from a Hindu majority country, where my identity had never been an issue. As the daughter of a clergyman, theological reflection came naturally to me, and from the first day, concepts of British ethnicity raised theological questions in my mind.

The Heathrow incident was not a one-off thing. Abuse on account of my ethnicity comes in many different ways. Someone might call out, 'Paki go home', a bottle might be thrown at me, I might be spat at or not served in a shop, department store assistants might follow me around assuming I was shop-lifting, people might presume that I didn't understand English and was stupid ... the list is endless. What is interesting for me is the realisation that the Church is no different. It often mirrors society's prejudices.

When Stephen was thinking of marrying me, a clergyman wrote to him, 'There might be a meeting of bodies, but would there be a meeting of minds?' We are both Christians and religious people why shouldn't there be a meeting of minds? After I arrived in Britain another clergyman thought he was being funny and said, 'Put away your foreign wives.' People just saw my Indian-ness, and refused to accept me as a fellow Christian. It is in the church that many people have expressed completely dualistic views about India and Britain: in every respect India is inferior and Britain is superior. I often wonder how people, who hardly know anything about India, can pass such irrational judgements. But then pride and prejudices are not based on facts.

My experience and the following verse shed light on each other: 'He has scattered the proud in the imagination of their heart' (Luke 1. 51 RSV). Human pride exists only in the imagination. The roots of such imaginary pride in British people can be found in the writings of the great giants of the European Enlightenment such as David Hume who declared, 'I am apt to suspect the Negroes and in general all other species of men (for there are four or five different kinds) to be naturally inferior to the whites.'

Our two sons were born; I knew that it would be harmful for them to be brought up in Britain. We looked for ways to leave the country. Stephen was invited by the Church of Bangladesh, initially to pastor the expatriate community in Dhaka. So we went. We as a family were foreigners in Bangladesh, but there my suffering on account of my ethnicity came, not from the Bangladeshis, but from the British expatriate community. I will just tell one story from that period.

One evening Stephen and I were at a party given by a British diplomat. At that gathering, somehow an inner circle developed which excluded me. A White British doctor, a rather quiet and shy person, also found himself excluded from the inner circle. Standing on the margin of the group we found each other and engaged in a conversation. After a while the host came to us and said to the doctor: 'Sorry to have left you all alone here.' I was shocked: all alone! What about me, was I invisible? The host managed to insult both of us. The doctor said, 'I am fine here talking with Mrs Barton' and we remained where we were. The diplomat, who could not see me, was a member of our church. I was his vicar's wife. We regularly worshipped together. I was really surprised that this diplomat could not see me. But it is common knowledge that power affects one's eyesight in a real sense. Powerful people sometimes cannot see the person they consider inferior. There are many biblical verses about this phenomenon of sighted people not being able to see. Jesus said, 'Do you have eyes, and fail to see?' (Mark 8. 18, NRSV).

Over the years I have noticed that White people are often in a state of cognitive dissonance, in a place of anxiety caused by the incongruity between what they have been indoctrinated to believe and what they actually see and hear. The incident at the party in the house of the diplomat is a case in point. In such parties, except for the servants, I used to be the only person of colour, invited as a White vicar's wife. My presence as an invited guest put the diplomat in a state of cognitive dissonance. He had two choices, either to discard his stereotypical belief about people like me, or not to see me at all. It was easier for him not to see me.

After being with many British people, who saw themselves as ethnically superior, I began to recognise the workings of power dynamics in relationships. However, the traditional theology that I knew could not provide me with any tools to respond theologically to oppression of the powerless by the powerful. This is the time Bangladeshi women began to invite me to their women's theological conferences. I came across Asian women's theology and then western feminist theology. I learned how to respond to gender based oppression, I honed my theological skills and founded a women's centre for doing theology for liberation and justice.

After eleven years in Bangladesh, we came back to Britain. I continued to find examples of cognitive dissonance. Christianity is the third major religion in India. Historically Indian Christianity is older than British Christianity. There are more Christians in India than in Britain. Yet to many British people 'Indian Christian' is a contradiction in terms. Generally in Britain people have been conditioned to believe that Indians are 'heathens'. When I meet Christians who do not know me, they invariably ask, 'What religion are you, a Hindu, a Muslim or a Sikh?' When I say, 'I am a Christian', the next question is, 'When were you converted?' These presumptions can wind me up a bit, but I continue to learn to respond to these questions without showing my irritation.

I gained more experience of cases of cognitive dissonance when we lived in a vicarage. When I answered the door, people often asked, 'Do you live here?' I wanted to say, 'No, I just sleep with the vicar,' but I never managed that.

Jesus said, 'Do you have ears, and fail to hear? (Mark 8. 18 NRSV). I have met people who have ears, but they cannot hear. One day I was in the front garden of the vicarage talking with our White neighbour over the fence. A White woman was passing and seeing me she said, 'This house used to be a vicarage.' Both our neighbour and I said several times, 'It still is a vicarage.' But she could not hear what we were saying. She went away muttering, 'It used to be a vicarage'. She saw me and could not believe that an Indian woman could have anything to do with a vicarage. Her prejudice was so much stronger than the truth that she could not hear it.

In Britain I wrote a thesis about my experience of theological work in Bangladesh and obtained a PhD. Following that, I began to teach Black and Asian theology from a colour and gender perspective in a theological college. One day during the Induction Week I led a service in the college chapel. After the service a new White student asked me, 'What religion are you?' He named all the religions except Christianity. Even after I had led a Christian service in a Christian worship place this White man still could not see me as a Christian.

When I teach theology, I realise that not only my ethnicity, but that of biblical people, including Jesus, also causes cognitive dissonance in the minds of White people. If Christians have been indoctrinated to believe 'all other species ... to be naturally inferior to the whites' (see above), then an African-Asiatic Jesus poses a huge challenge to that belief. The only option left is to turn Jesus into a White man. In India British Christianity taught us to believe that White people were superior to us and that Jesus was White. The myth of White Jesus continues to be perpetuated through many things such as stained-glass windows, biblical films, theological book covers, Christmas and other religious cards. Once I preached a sermon from a colour and race perspective in a church and then when I was distributing communion, a man refused to take the chalice from me, shouted and stormed out of the church.

After living in Britain since 1975, teaching hundreds of students in a theological college for 16 years, working in many churches for 12 years, I have come to recognise that the White superiority complex has seriously distorted the truth about humanity, the Bible and Jesus and divided the world on colour/ethnic lines. If we really want to deal with this serious world issue, a lot of time has to be given to systematic awareness-building processes. Since in the theological college I have this time, I have more success here than in churches. Many of my students are ordinands. After being in my class many of them begin to see what they did not see before and become agents of change in their churches. It is a great pity that most theological colleges are not teaching theology from ethnic and colour perspectives in a systematic way.

Sometimes I think if I had not come to Britain, I would not have faced the storms of racism and my life would have been much nicer. Then I look back and reflect deeply. Before I came I was happy in my Indian identity. I had no reason to ask questions about the ideas of superiority and inferiority or to challenge the myth of a White Jesus.

Then came the storms of racism and shattered my known identity. I had to ask, 'Who am I'? And, 'Who are you, God?' Through the questioning and searching I realised that all human beings are created in God's own image and that the myth of superiority and inferiority is contradictory to biblical teachings. Now I have a stronger sense of my identity and know that people who are proud in their imagination are living dangerously. I recognise that whiteness is not superior and that Jesus did not come into the world as a White man. Jesus said, 'you will know the truth, and the truth will make you free.' (John 8:32, NRSV). I have seen people becoming free when they discard the imaginary world and learn to live in the real world.

The storm of racism shattered my doors and through the broken doors God-as-truth came in to fill my emptiness. I would like to end with a song of Rabindranath Tagore that I have translated from Bengali:

The night when the storm shattered my
    doors.
Unaware I was
it was you, you who came into my home,

the night when the storm shattered my
	doors.

All went dark, my lamp went out.
I stretched out my arms to the sky.
Who was I reaching out to?
Unaware I was
it was you, you who came into my home,
the night when the storm shattered my
	doors.

I lay in the dark thinking it was a dream.
Little did I know
that the storm was heralding you.
Then came the dawn and I looked up:
there you were, standing,
standing over the emptiness that had filled
	my home.

Unaware I was
it was you, you who came into my home,
the night when the storm shattered my
	doors.

Notes

David Hume cited in *Emmanuel Chukwudi
Eze, Race and Enlightenment: A Reader*,
Oxford: Blackwell, 1997, p. 33.

Scott's story

Scott Rennie is a Church of Scotland Minister at Queen's Cross Church, Aberdeen. He has studied at the University of Aberdeen and Union Theological Seminary in New York. Scott was a member of the Church of Scotland's Taskforce on Human Sexuality. In 2009 Scott was nominated for, and subsequently won, the award of 'Hero of the Year' at the Fourth Annual Stonewall Awards. He is a keen supporter of Aberdeen Football Club, aka 'The Dons'.

I imagine that for many others, like me, who tick the box 'white British' on any survey, ethnicity has never been much of an issue or point of discussion. When faced with the term 'ethnicity' I used to think of others – black Caribbean or African, Asian, Latino/a. Growing up in the north east of Scotland I certainly never imagined that ethnicity was a category that included me. Now in my forties, the familiar cultural world in which I grew up and in which my identity was formed looks different, and it has made me think differently about ethnicity later in life.

Like everyone else the factors which moulded my sense of identity and ethnicity began in childhood. Like nearly everyone who grew up in my white working class community my family were adherents of (if not always enthusiastic members) of the Kirk – the white Presbyterian and Protestant Church of Scotland. I grew up British and Scottish (in that order) and even through the Thatcher years, that order and national identity was never in question. I remember every Friday evening at Boys Brigade, the National Anthem being plinked out on the piano, and the Union Flag being raised while we saluted. Little did I know that in other parts of Scotland (the sectarian divided West) this would have been viewed by some as a highly politicised activity. I didn't meet my first Roman Catholic until I was in my teens, and even then the fact that she was called Teresa was no clue to me of her Roman Catholic family background. In any case, happily it was something that none of us thought about, or could have cared less about.

In a secondary school of 900 pupils everyone was white – except for one Chinese boy, who spoke English anyway. I was glad to call him my friend for as long as he was with us in school, his ethnicity was not really of any interest or novelty. Basically being British and white was such a 'given' in my childhood and adolescence, in a largely white city of 200,000 like Aberdeen, that ethnicity was something that always applied to someone else who was different or whose origins seemed to lie somewhere else. Talk of ethnicity was distant.

It was a postgraduate year of study in the ethnic melting pot of New York City in my mid-twenties that awakened me to my own sense of also being part of a minority. My year of postgraduate theological study at the marvellous and diverse Union Theological Seminary in the city took the scales off my eyes. My denominational and theological assumptions were revealed to me. Life in New York City as a Brit abroad also revealed to me how different I was, even to other white people (Americans), not to mention people from other cultures from around the globe, all of whom had found a resting place in that great place. Ex-pat Scots, whom I sought out for some comfort, appeared in their exile more Scottish than even I, revelling in a kind of Scotto nostalgia born of separation and distance. So much so, that all of the tartan and romanticism made me feel queasy.

In 1999 I returned home to work as a minister of the national church, still a large and influential institution in Scottish society, though diminished somewhat in its cultural dominance, even since my childhood in the late 1970s and in the 1980s. By the end of the 1990s cultural assumptions in Scotland were changed, largely through secularisation. There was an increase in the number of Scots belonging to ethnic minorities, as well as the political ascendancy of Scottish Nationalism.

All over Europe a desire for localism, and a greater political expression of nationalism and ethnicity has been on the rise. This is also true of Catalonia, the Basque country, Eastern Europe with the fall of the Iron Curtain, not only Scotland. Not only that, but political nationalism in Scotland has been able to embrace the ethnic and cultural diversity of modern Scotland, in a way that the white protestant Scottish/British culture I grew up in struggled to do. It is sometimes described as 'civic nationalism' and it has undoubtedly transcended sectarian and cultural divides.

The current culture of modern Scotland while it still wrestles with the many divides in Scottish life, at least, post-devolution has taken the challenge on. For example, I think of the ease with which Equal Marriage recently became law, something that would have been unthinkable in my childhood. I see the many diverse colours of faces and accents in the Scottish Parliament, something else in which I take pride. Some years ago this cultural shift in public life was summed up in a Scottish Executive campaign: 'One Scotland – Many Cultures'.

I am proud of a civic society in which someone of Pakistani descent growing up in Glasgow is recognised to be no less Scottish than I am, and yet I would be lying if I were to pretend that the transition to realising my own culture as one among many, has been without a sense of loss. This pain or sense of loss is nothing however to the regret I feel that my own Church has been unable to embrace diversity in terms of sexuality, unlike the wider society in which resides.

In this journey of self-revelation, where I have come to see myself as belonging to one cultural and ethnic strand in the tapestry that makes up modern Scotland, I have one lingering worry – around political nationalism. I grew up British and Scottish; I continue to see no conflict between the two, and I feel an enduring loyalty to both. I take exception to the suggestion by some of my peers that the two are exclusionary. I enjoy being Scottish,

British and European, and I believe Scotland is enriched by this multiple sense of identity that individuals in other Scottish communities experience to different expressions of nationality as well.

Post-referendum Scotland is changed. Many good and valued friends tell me their nationalism is a civic and inclusive one. Up to a point it may well be, and on their part I have no doubt it is. However, though they may be a small fringe element, nonetheless I hear the voices that denigrate the English and things British, even if in jocular fashion; and I see the saltires that wave, for me, in an exclusionary fashion. It sits uncomfortably with me, however much for many my concerns would appear overblown and out of proportion.

For me, the journey of discovery through which I have come to see my own particular place in the world, culturally and ethnically, has been one in which I have been enabled to rejoice in diversity, and my bit part in it. It would be horrible to see one exclusionary environment, after years of progress, replaced by another, however subtle and non-offensive a brave new Scotland may at first appear. In short, I distrust nationalism for the lines it inevitably draws between different people, however well intentioned. But that is just me.

One thing is sure, all my white British assumptions are up for question in modern Scotland. I am glad to have been made aware of my partial and small part in the cultural tapestry of modern Scotland, for sure. How the British/Scottish question will end, I am more nervous about.

PART 2

Theology

A Theology of Ethnicity
MICHAEL JAGESSAR

Each book in this series contains a substantial theological reflection by an expert in the field. Here Michael Jagessar challenges us to consider how the church could be a 'rainbow tapestry'; and encourages us to consider accepting the invitation to dance with God.

MICHAEL JAGESSAR is a minister of the United Reformed Church (UK) with responsibility for intercultural theology and practice of ministry. Michael is the immediate past moderator of the General Assembly of the United Reformed Church (2012–2014). He has taught ecumenical theology, interfaith studies, Black and contextual theologies and practice, liturgy and worship and practical theology. In the Caribbean Michael has been involved in a variety of ministries, including community development work in Guyana and Grenada and ecumenical theological education in Guyana, Grenada and Curacao. He has written extensively and more on his work and publications can be found on his webpage (www.caribleaper.co.uk). Michael locates himself as member of the Caribbean diaspora who embodies multiple identities and for whom 'home' is always elsewhere!

CHAPTER 1

Rainbow Tapestry (or God's Mosaic): towards a theology of ethnicity

Introducing our conversation: reality check and key question

Have you ever noticed the number of churches and/or communities describing themselves as multicultural or multi-ethnic, listing the mind-boggling number of ethnicities that make-up their community? Our world, our nation, and our communities are rapidly changing around us. Our trans-global/local world and the fact of massive movements of people for a variety of reasons mean that societies that used to be perceived as homogenous have become more aware of the ethnic and cultural diversity in their midst. Globalization also means that immigrants and refugees are bringing their customs and traditions right to our doorstep. More than ever before, the nations are a mosaic of different ethnicities. They are nations within nations and we are becoming more aware of this. The 2011 Census (UK) noted that ethnic groups, other than White British, accounted for 20% of the population of England and Wales, compared to 14% in 2001. Among the population other than White British or Irish, there was a particular increase amongst the ethnic groups such as Africans, Chinese, Bangladeshi and Pakistanis. While growth can be linked to their youthful populations, there is also the matter of continuing immigration to the UK and a growing 'mixed' ethnic identity population. In fact, 'mixed ethnic' groups as a whole in the UK, increased by more than 80% and now include over a million people.

This changing landscape has resulted in a shifting discourse where there is now more awareness of one's roots and ethnic origin as we strive to build a common life together and as the nature of English-ness, Scottish-ness and Welsh-ness is being re-configured and re-negotiated on this new terrain. The recent Scottish referendum highlighted this. But while some of these discourses have been positive, there is also the reality of fear, xenophobia and ethnic bashing as 'native' purists argue that their identity is being compromised and even disappearing, though still in a majority.

Given all our good intentions of being

inclusive communities, what in reality does it mean for the body of Christ to live out the good news of abundant life for all in our multi-everything world? This is the urgent question before us in this changing context. For the greatest challenge to making the gospel real and living in our post-everything world may well include crossing the 'distance' of ethnicity, race and culture more so than that of geography and economics. In a time of increased ethnic strife, xenophobia and migrant scapegoating across all political colours, how will Christians in the UK and beyond respond? Will we be bewildered onlookers to the reality of ethnic multiplicity? Will we welcome this enormous blessing of the ethnic mix of nations and cultures as God's gift of our rainbow world to us? The challenge is not necessarily difference as this is the reality of our contexts. Differences such as ethnicity, gender and orientation disclose the richness of the manifoldness of God. However, the staggering diversity of our current reality will continue to overwhelm our theological senses, unless we stop and seek to better understand from scripture about God's plan and purpose for ethnic diversity. And the church urgently needs to revisit and draw from its 'treasures' to articulate a theology of ethnicity.

What is ethnicity?

Discussions of ethnicity are prone to misunderstanding so it is important that we clarify what we mean by it. What is ethnicity's relationship to race, culture and nationalism? Depending on one's status, allegiances, relative position, and reason for group identification, ethnicity will be described variously. While the term has its roots in the Greek word *ethnos* or *ethnikos* meaning a large group of people bound together by the same manners, customs or other distinctive features, ethnicity has a relatively recent history.[9]

In its simplest form an ethnic group is identified by one or more of the categories of race, religion, and national origin. Hence, membership for some is usually determined by birth if ethnicity is closely related to the idea of one's ancestral background.[10] As a result of an intentional construct, ethnicity points to a shared/common cultural heritage, common

[9] The term first appeared in the dictionary in 1953 though it seems to have entered modern discourse in 1941 when introduced to study largely 'white' European immigrants to the United States as an alternative to the term 'race'. Ethnicity first appeared in a dictionary in 1953 and as a widespread analytical concept in the social sciences around the 1960s, mainly resulting from Fredrik Barth's seminal essay on ethnicity in 1969!

[10] Tamotsu Shibutani and Kian M. Kwan, *Ethnic Stratification: A Comparative Approach* (New York: Macmillan, 1965), 47.

ancestry, history, language, nationality or
religion which will give people a unique
social identity.[11] While such self-conscious
identification includes: physical features,
common ancestry, shared historical memories,
symbols, traditions, link with a geographical
location and language,[12] it is not necessarily
limited to these nor depends on all of these.[13]
Thus some[14] often speak of ethnic thickness or
thinness to underscore the importance or not of
a person's location with a particular group.

In our multicultural societies ethnicity is
perhaps more fluid, dynamic and expansive
than in traditional societies where it is more
exclusive. So ethnicity, while related to
race, refers more to social traits (not only
physical features) that are shared by a human
population. In some instances, ethnicity may

[11] See, J.J. Macionis, *Sociology* 15th Edition (Upper Saddle
River, NJ: Prentice Hall, 2010); Sze-kar Wan, 'To the Jew
First and also to the Greek': Reading Romans as Ethnic
Construction' [129-155] in Laura Nasrallah and Elisabeth
Schussler Fiorenza (editors), *Prejudice and Christian
Beginnings: Investigating Race, Gender, and ethnicity in
Early Christian Studies* (Minneapolis: Fortress Press, 2009)

[12] See, Linbert Spencer, *Building a Multi-Ethnic Church*
(London: SPCK, 2007).

[13] Stephen Cornell and Douglas Hartmann, *Ethnicity and
Race: Making Identities in a Changing World* 2nd edition.
(Thousand Oaks, CA: Pine Forge, 2007)

[14] Cornell and Hartmann, *Ethnicity and Race*, pp. 85–89.

refer to a loose group identity with little or no cultural traditions in common. In contrast, some ethnic groups are subcultures with a shared language and body of tradition (for instance, newly arrived migrants). Ethnic groups may be either a minority or a majority in a population.

What is significant for our purpose is that the framing of 'ethnicity' is undergoing constant change. In many disciplines the complexity of the politics of representation has led to a questioning of the use of old 'binaries', or ways of defining categories as opposites and setting them off against each other (e.g. black/white; gay/straight; male/female). It is the case, for instance, that in our context (UK) the dominant group tends not to self-represent itself in ethnic terms. Thus, it is not uncommon in any form of monitoring of the diverse make-up in our Churches to face resistance from the dominant group both to provide the information or to see themselves as ethnic. Responses such as 'we are all Christians worshipping here' are not uncommon. So whether in church or society this often results in the 'invisibility' of the majority population with its cultural artefacts, shared narratives, history and language (etc.). And when ethnicity is largely identified with minority groups, there is the reality that these are often perceived through their 'otherness or foreignness'. This raises a whole heap of questions around a common 'belonging' in our life together.

Ethnicity, race and culture: a complex relationship:

Ethnicity, race and culture have, and continue to be, the subject of much debate. Scholars and practitioners have found it difficult to isolate or separate one from the other, arguing that these categories overlap or are interconnected. These markers shape or make our identity. They are powerful forces in our lives and the relationship is quite complex. The terms tend to be used interchangeably and, while meanings may overlap, each has its distinctive meaning(s) and history. Race, for instance, is often used in two ways: referring to common genetic characteristics of humankind (e.g. human race); or is used to highlight so-called differences between groups of humans (e.g. European race and African race). While the former underscores our common humanity, the latter stresses differences often leading to a hierarchy and consequently an oppressive binary of 'superior and inferior' groups of human beings. Unlike race, ethnicity is often seen to encompass both cultural and physical aspects of difference.[15] Now, how these terms are deployed can enlighten as they can add to confusion. It is sometimes difficult to distinguish between ethnic and racial prejudice. For instance, is prejudice against the Roma related to their construction as a 'racial' or as an 'ethnic' group? Does it have more to do with their presumed biological make up or with their cultural traditions? While recognising the complexities, what is important for our purpose are the multiple and complex ways ethnicity, race and culture intersect (function and interact). This is true of us today as it was for those of biblical times. We need to remember this in our God-talk or theologising.

The intersecting raises a number of questions. We note two: firstly, there is a current and prevailing tendency in the UK and Europe of putting the nation, national interest or state first, appealing to patriotism (whether British-ness or European-ness) or putting the individual's right first. This can easily lead to the domestication of one's ethnicity or ancestral cultures and subsuming all in a national identity that often favours the dominant

[15] Sujit Sivasundaram, 'Unity and Diversity: the church, race and ethnicity' in *Cambridge Papers: Towards a Biblical Mind 17/4 (December 2008), p.2 [1-4]*

group. The second is related to the question: who are ethnic? Is it only the minorities with their resistant strategies against the dominant group? Should not the native majority and the ways they respond to the newer 'ethnic other' be also seen as ethnic? Ethnic invisibility of the dominant group must not be underestimated. The fact that ethnicity is a collective construct located around a specific set of cultural markers, clearly suggests that native Brits (with their own multiplicity) are also ethnic. They, like other dominant groups, may not wish to see this or represent themselves this way. It is often the case that the dominant native population (e.g. Britain's English natives, Britain's Welsh natives, Britain's Scottish natives) often come to grips with their own identity and ethnic boundaries as a result of the presence of visible ethnic and racialized minorities.

So it is the case that 'ethnic fencing' runs across all groups: those at the top aiming to maintain their position of privilege; those at the bottom resisting all marginalising pressures and those in the middle navigating dual contestations directed at both. What this suggests is that ethnicity, class struggle, and race issues have an intertwining relationship with a critical dimension being the tendency to preserve one's own interests and privileges while ensuring that others do not transgress them. Very often this struggle is related to the sharing of (perceived) scarce resources. The current political discourse to the challenges posed by ethnic minority groups highlights this (subtly and, at times, overtly). This is reflected in the immigration policies of all our political parties as they attempt to win votes. And, one of the resulting fallouts is that ethnicity can be seen as contributing to growing polarisations across all walks of life.

Why a theology of Ethnicity?

In working towards a theology of ethnicity, there is a shape to our orienting premise. It is the premise that all societies are culturally plural (subtle and overt) even if there are a distinctive set of cultural conventions. In the most homogeneous looking societies, identities and the self-presentations vary from context to context. We are all embodied beings (ethnic, racial and cultural) operating from particular places, contexts and experiences. Who we are, our subjectivity, cannot be separated from our ethnic identities which are predicated on difference and diversity. How then do we do theology (that is our God-talk) in such a plural, complex, intersecting world as ours? What are the implications for our life together? Why the need to consider a theology of ethnicity?

If our commitment to diversity is to move beyond good intentions then relationships across racial, ethnic and cultural across boundaries is critical.[16] This means that an inclusive church needs to reframe its God-talk around ethnicity and its intersections. A theological consideration of ethnicity, however, necessitates in the first instance some reflection on biblical underpinnings.

Biblically speaking

We are creatures of the earth – interconnected and interdependent – reflecting God's diversity. From the beginning, diversity (not homogeneity) has been God's intention. The creation accounts suggest a God of extravagant goodness sculpting a multi layered, colourful and diverse world. That diversity is created of every kind, and though different, there is sense of unity, equality and interdependency. These early records of our sacred texts also show that humankind has been created in the image and likeness of the Divine Lover to be in communion. This is the biblical and theological basis for our life together.

[16] Sheryl A. Kujawa-Holbrook, *A House of Prayer for all Peoples: Congregations building Multicultural Community* (Virginia: The Alban Institute, 2002), 36.

So a cursory look at the Hebrew Bible underscores humanity's inter-connectedness in the image and likeness of God. By the time we get to Sarah and Abraham, we become aware of groups of people, nations and cultures. It is significant that, very early on, the biblical story-tellers present us with stories of migration and the meeting and interacting of cultures. It is not unreasonable to deduce from reading through the Hebrew Bible (often referred to as the Old Testament) that there are a number of insights on ethnicity, culture and diversity. Recent re-readings of the Babel story, for instance, affirm diversity as something that serves the purposes of God for the human family. There is a sense of affirmation that diversity of cultures, nations, groups, languages and ethnicities is an essential part of the biblical stories. This includes the reality of interacting, border crossings, competition, conflict, and trading, etc. And, while Israel's chosen-ness complicates and highlights the tensions around ethnicity and inclusion, the scriptures are laced with examples of how notions of purity have been compromised by exile, interacting and intermarrying. At the same time, God (that is the God of Israel) is also a God of nations and people.[17]

[17] Isaiah 45:1-7.

So to absolutize one's own nation or group, whether it takes the form of xenophobia, ethno-centrism or excluding nationalism, is a distortion of God's plan – both a negation of our inter-relationship and a lie about God. God's covenanted relationship with Israel is one example (in our view a proto-type) through which God's grace could reach out and bless all nations (the vision as captured in Revelation). This purpose was made explicit in the call God gave to Abraham: 'all peoples on earth will be blessed through you'. And God's purpose included both the physical and spiritual welfare of all people. This is displayed in God's ample provision made for the foreigner/alien/immigrant. Strangers in the midst of God's people were to be loved in the name of the triune God who loves strangers. All were to be embraced and welcomed by the people of God. Holiness and hospitality, reflecting the very character and nature of God, were both to characterize the covenanted people of God in their relationships with all.

This theme flows into and through the New Testament. The ministry of Jesus, a Jew with a Galilean accent[18], is replete with examples of expansive generosity that transgressed narrow boundaries. It is a ministry of including, giving agency to diversity, building

[18] Matthew 24:73.

inclusive community and crossing/re-crossing geographical, national, cultural and ethnic boundaries. What is clear from Jesus' ministry is that God shows no partiality except, perhaps, a preference for those forced on the periphery. For Jesus as a Jew, ethnicity matters though his message moves beyond the enclave of his ethnic, cultural and religious group. Eugene Peterson's version of John 1:14 is apt: 'The Word became flesh and blood, and moved into the neighbourhood'.[19] Interestingly, in spite of this and the great emphasis placed on the incarnation, there has been little or no attention given to a theology of ethnicity.

The birth of the Christian community (the people of the way) at Pentecost affirms ethnic, linguistic and cultural diversity. The Holy Spirit descends in the tongues of the different nations, enabling friends and followers of Jesus to speak in a variety of languages. The new religious movement would not make ethnic homogeneity the price of admission. Instead it deploys a common message to increasingly distant and variegated people. In Acts 16, for instance, Luke chooses not to neglect or reject the presence and importance of ethnic boundaries, but to find ways to challenge

[19] *The Message: The Bible in Contemporary Language* (Navpress: Colorado, 2002).

them and exploit them for his theological purposes. Providing a theological narrative of the spread of the Christian gospel throughout the Mediterranean world required the author to grapple with its ethnic diversity.

At the heart of the early church's story is ethnicity, cultures and nations as the Christian faith begins as a movement within first century Judaism, with the first followers all Jews and then crossing the geographical borders of the world of Palestine. Not surprisingly, an early question these Jesus followers faced was whether the good news about Jesus was only for the Jews or was it also for all the 'others' – the gentiles? In various ways, this tension is also there in the four gospel accounts.[20] The inclusive message and expansive embrace of the good news of Jesus is even more evident in the Acts of the Apostles with Luke underscoring that Jesus' offer of abundant life (salvation) is for all people through faith.[21]

Considering Acts as a case study in the rich ethnic diversity of God's people remains an exciting and revealing exercise for us today. For what we find here are stories of the incursion of the gospel transgressing borders

[20] Matthew 1:1-16; 2:1-12; 8:5-13; Cf. Matthew 15:24; 28:19; John 4; Luke 10:29-37.

[21] Acts 2; 8:26-40; 10:15.

and boundaries, and an invitation to enter worlds in which ethnic difference and diversity are held in the many-one-ness of the Christian faith. Acts does not erase ethnic difference but employs the flexible bounds of ethnicity in order to illustrate the wide demographic ambitions of the early church movement, but also the uneasy negotiations of ethnicity such a movement would require. In Romans and Galatians we find a concrete example of wrestling with the implications of the gospel's radical grace and the historic claims of Israel, and Paul's conclusion that there is no longer Jew nor Greek.[22] God's desire is to create a new community grounded in God's expansive love for all. This is often repeated throughout the pastoral letters. So in Revelation, we find the gathering – the twelve tribes of Israel and a multitude of people of all cultures and languages, too many to count, around the throne of God in one praise.[23]

The foregoing is merely a selective glance at the bible. What it shows, however, is that human beings in their diversity have been part of God's embrace, perhaps on the same grounds that Abraham and Sarah were justified, by faith.

[22] Galatians 3:28.

[23] Revelation 7:9.

Ethnicity matters. In the Hebrew Scriptures, 'nations' may be equated with what, we today, would present as 'ethnic groups' rather than political communities (modern 'nation states'). Biblical 'nations' may have common names, cultures, homelands, and a sense of solidarity. And various terms, thick with meanings, were used to designate the elastic concept of ethnicity: families/clans, tribes, nations, and peoples. While God may have chosen the Hebrews (later becoming the nation of Israel) as family, it was one in which the story became complicated through the presence of ethnic 'others', such as Jethro, Rahab, Naaman, Ruth, and Uriah, ultimately becoming part of that story.[24]

Matthew's gospel account takes this up through his 'theological genealogy' to establish Jesus' legitimacy as being of the lineage of David and Abraham. (Matthew 1). In that list are five women who have transgressed a significant number of the established 'border-rules' intended to control ethnic cross-over. In fact, the first four were not of Israelite origin and read alongside John Agard's satirical poem 'Half-Caste', a satirical take on the notion of purity, makes for an interesting juxtaposed conversation! Matthew takes theology back to

---

[24] See, Milton Acosta Benítez, 'Ethnicity and the People of God' in *Theologica Xaveriana* 59/168 (2009)319 [309-330].

context – its ethnic location – as he makes his case for the Jesus way of abundant life for all. This is full life that highlights the specificity of one's ethnic, race and culture. This is full life that transcends any ethnocentric tendencies that would claim that particular beliefs, cultural perspectives and points of view are better and superior to others; transforming them to something larger than each distinctive identity. It is an invitation to the poly-ethnic and varied world of God in Christ where we do not become disembodied ethnic and cultural beings; but where life in Christ is re-shaped and re-negotiated according to kingdom values.

Scripture speaks of one-humanity characterised by multiplicity and created by God. It recounts our rebellion and tells of a diverse people reconciled to God through Christ, a people set free for the work of reconciliation. It heralds a new freedom and future in the many-one-ness of God in Christ. The Holy Spirit breathes the freedom of the gospel into the church, where every people under heaven is represented. Cultural differences still matter, but they can be seen for what God intends – blessing rather than means of enslavement and exclusion.

For God so loved the world (of many peoples, tribes, tongues, cultures, nations) ... Some theological touchstones

Theology, or more precisely God-talk, is always a work of faith inseparable from the lived experiences of the everyday life and ought to point towards liberative transformation. Such embodying of theology can never claim to be objective, especially if objectivity means keeping a safe emotional and cognitive distance from the subject matter and/or a neutral stance. We are involved and implicated. Our God-talk, whatever form or shape it takes, will reflect the ethnicity, gender, sexual orientation, culture, and socio/economic location (*inter alia*) that have shaped and continue to shape us. This is besides the fact that our received texts (whether the bible or doctrines/traditions) are already culturally and ideologically conditioned. In our God-talk nothing falls into our lap out of 'cloud nine'. I am yet to meet a disembodied theologian though quite a few may operate as if they are. We all read, listen and do our God-talk with a view. This is especially the case for people for whom God is not a theological dictum but intimately involved in their lives as marginalised people.

Ethnicity is a fact which the church cannot ignore. As a movement, the early Christian community emerged in contexts characterised by a high degree of ethnic, cultural and religious diversity. A sense of collective identity is an inherent element in human nature. Our humanness is inevitably diminished when we do not pay attention to this reality. In fact, it may be the case that denial of ethnicity, race and culture (or diversity) leads to our dehumanising tendencies. In our ecclesial life, ethnicity constitutes an opportunity and enrichment to our life together. God, from what our scriptures reveal, affirms our distinctiveness, ethnic and cultural embodiment. Differences and diversity are not intended to shape a world of insiders and outsiders as this distorts God's purpose. Yet, while a vision of unity and (ethnic) diversity should not be at odds or mutually excluding, the reality from the time of the early church to this day is that the church struggles to make sense of ethnic diversity. Ethnic diversity is a theological virtue and the prejudices and discrimination that are associated with ethnicity is a betrayal of God's plan for a diverse world. What, from our brief glance into the biblical narratives, can we discern as a number of possible theological underpinnings for us to consider?

CHAPTER 2

Diversity –
God's way in Christ

Our creation in the image of God has to be our starting point. This is foundational to our God-talk. We are created as neighbours to live in communities. Locating ethnicity in the divine image provides a biblical, sociological, and theological foundation for multi ethnic church communities and our intercultural life together. The implication here is the human race is one. All the diverse people of earth of whatever ethnicity belong to one family. This means that God is the God of all people everywhere, whether they know this or not. Because we all have our identity in and through God (made in God's image) it means that every human being is our brother and sister. This equality in the sight of the divine then makes any form of dehumanisation of another being or groups of people a distortion of God's purpose. This 'sin' is what some refer to as 'the negation of relation' or as a 'lie'. Both obscure the particularity and equal worth of the other. No individual or ethnic group should entertain notions of superiority.

This may have been in the mind of Paul when he addressed the Athenians: 'From one ancestor [God] made all nations to inhabit the whole earth, and [God] allotted the times of their existence and the boundaries of the places where they would live'. If only our live-out God-talk could reflect this or even have an awareness of this, then we could at least have a moral and spiritual platform to collectively stand on to work towards ending the evil consequences of the idolatry of ethnocentrism and racism.

God is love, and there is a unity of love in the person of God – creator, redeemer, and sustainer. Out of this overflowing love, God chose to create a world that is wonderfully varied. There is 'oneness' and 'many-one-ness'. Nowhere in the scriptures can one glean a sense of God desiring uniformity. Diversity is an inherent feature of God's purpose – not as a consequence of missing the mark (sin). It is Divine intention. The whole creation witnesses to the fact that God enjoys diversity, and different ethnic groups are but one expression of this divine joy.

Ethnic diversity offers a context for the flowering of human creativity. The cultural variety fostered by a multiplicity of people channels the creative impulses of humanity into numerous and widely diverse streams. Consequently, ethnic difference is a potential source of mutual enrichment. Besides, multiplicity of people serves to contain human pride and evil on a global scale and has done so throughout history. Over-powerful and totalising regimes are restrained and brought down by other people who are threatened by and stand up to them. In other words, ethnicity serves as a brake on certain forms of human sin and their potential to cause limitless evil.

As we have noted, God's focus on Sarah and Abraham is intended to be a blessing to the nations. This becomes evident as the story of God's salvific purpose unfolds with constant reminders of how every attempt towards homogeneity or drawing boundaries is 'adulterated' or transgressed by ethnic and cultural cross-overs. God's purpose is that a variety of people would make-up the world. It is difficult to imagine that God desires homogeneity or uniformity for individuals or groups. The many-one-ness of humanity underscores God's preference for multiplicity in togetherness. It also reflects the manifoldness of God's infinity: variety offers us a glimpse of the Divine, with each part mirroring an aspect of the beauty/majesty of the 'holy other' and each needing the other to point to the greater goodness of God the extravagant lover. This is also evident in the ministry of Jesus and the story of early followers of Jesus, as we have noted.

God's purpose for all nations includes a future eschatological kingdom. The bible is replete with promises and predictions that one day all nations will make pilgrimage to Zion to learn about the ways of God – especially the psalms. This ingathering is depicted as an eschatological event, initiated by God. It appears that this coming kingdom will be twofold: on earth and yet also eternal in the new heaven and earth. In the future age, God will initiate a new covenant where all ethnic nations – will be incorporated into the new people of God. To appreciate the way in which ethnic identity is blessed by God, it is illuminating to consider how the word 'nation' is used in the bible. It is not just isolated individuals that enter the kingdom but nations in all their variety and with all their distinctive treasures. Nationhood has an eschatological value.

Diversity is God's blessing for the enrichment of the church's life together – a visible expression of the shape of God's realm. Thus, the image of God in us is most fully realized in the context of a diverse and loving community[25] where we learn from those whose experiences, beliefs, and perspectives are different from our own. The witness of churches (its message lived out) carries integrity and credibility when the world sees Christians growing and deepening relationships regardless of ethnicity and culture. We strive after the 'not yet' that one day all will be reconciled back to God in Christ. It may have been this vision that John on Patmos saw.[26] When Christians understand and embrace the value God places on diversity, then the likelihood that the fear of knowing and being known by others disappears. Then we realize that diversity is the norm, not the exception, in God's kingdom. The vision of heaven is to affect our reality now. Authentic living is found in our connectedness – our life together. In fact, the need to belong to a group is wired deeply into our psyche. And the meaning and purpose of human life is best realised in the relational context of our life together. This places a high value on diversity within the one human family. Diversity is not a barrier to the expansive embrace of God's love. It simply serves a redemptive purpose in God's plan.

[25] I Corinthians 12.

[26] Revelations 7:9.

CHAPTER 3

Incarnation, ethnic self and embodied God-talk

A theology of ethnicity must find a home in the incarnation. God assumed human form in Christ to heal and save all humankind. But this universal reach of the incarnation must be seen for its particularity. It happened in a specific country, among a specific people and at a specific moment. The incarnate Christ assumed the totality of human nature while at the same time becoming an individual person belonging to a distinct ethnic group – Jewish. He assumed ethnicity. In so doing, Christ has blessed the distinct and particular identity of each human being and, by extension, of each nation. In this way the incarnation embraces human nature in its universality while affirming the different expressions of that one nature in all their variety and specificity.

Ethnicity does play a role in the heritage of

Jesus, a Galilean Jew, with a remarkable list of the hybrid mix in his bloodline that punctures insistence on the nonsense of purity! In a way Jesus both transcends and dismantles race and ethnicity as our ideal multiple identity person. And so in the world of the early church and pastoral letters the multi-ethnic Jesus becomes the one to help people to transcend their narrow dividing of groups while honouring their respective identities. In Christ, we all experience 'mutual inconveniencing', becoming a 'new creation'! Yet, in spite of this and the loads we have written over the years about the incarnation and even sing over and over in hymns, we still find it difficult to embrace and welcome the 'other' who is embodied different from us.

One of the strategies of the dominant group is to encourage a disembodied discourse which means that, if it is spirituality of theology, the ethnic self with its affections and physicality is not given agency either in constructing our self-understanding or imagining who God is and how God is present in our lives and world. The complex and intersecting differences of race, ethnicity, gender, orientation, culture, and class are integral to our embodied experience. Embodiment can become a powerful theological and pastoral resource for our work of countering exclusive and oppressive practices

Many-one-ness in Christ

So how does one claim one's ethnic identity in the context of a universal claim of Christianity as 'racially inclusive? In contexts where race consciousness plays a central role in the theological constructions of racially marginalized and oppressed communities, how do we make sense of ethnic particularity within the church's theological formulations? How do we re-read the interpretative tendencies of Paul's oneness theory that we are all 'one in Christ'? How do I, as an Indo-Caribbean being, claim my ethnic identity in my self-understanding and practice of Christian identity? Does unity in Christ matter so much that my individuality, ethnic and cultural heritages must be forfeited for me to become one in Christ or a new 'creation' in Christ?

One of the challenges in inclusive church and racial justice work in churches is how to get Christian communities to resist quick attempts at subsuming all under the banner of 'one love', 'one in Christ' or some form of 'sameness' agenda. Familiar biblical texts that tend to quickly gloss over differences and move to an unreal and homogenous 'oneness in Christ' is unfaithful to diversity. One possible reason is that the dominant group (for example White English, Welsh or Scottish) as a racial/

ethnic identity is never implicated. Such ex-
nomination of the dominant group as ethnic
identity entertains the view that ethnicity
or difference lives 'out there'. An absence/
presence model of ethnicity neglects to explore
privilege and leaves power invisible. In the
process, cultural and ethnic specificities are
denied and subsumed under the so-called
Pauline formula. A theology of ethnicity must
expose the limitations and interpretative
practices of 'being one in Christ' especially its
capacity to serve the interest of the dominant
group/culture. We need to be aware of how our
deploying of 'one in Christ', 'one bread' and 'one
body' can become a tool to erase difference or
ethnicity.

Being united in Christ through faith does
not mean that ethnic and cultural differences
will be erased or dissolved. Rather, ethnic and
other categories are no longer definitive of our
identities. 'There is neither Jew nor Greek,
slave nor free, male nor female, for you are
all one in Christ Jesus' (Galatians 3:28) is
not a call to erase ethnic, class, and gender
diversity in an absolute sense. Rather, it is a
call to break down any existing barriers and
inequalities between them. In our specific case,
it is about how to be church – members of the
body of Christ! Viewed through a hospitality

lens, it is in encounter of being guests and hosts to one another's differences that we are 'one in Christ'. Hence diversity is affirmed and named without collapsing difference into a prescription for becoming like us.

If ethnicity is understood differently, is it possible that we can read passages such as Galatians 3:28 to affirm hybridity and differences? Instead of binaries of either/or, how about both/and metaphors for mixture or hybridity, that is the straddling of multiple identities and belonging? Can this help us to overcome the prioritising of being in Christ that side line various identities: Judean, Greek, slave, free, male, female, etc? It is a mistake to prioritise unity over multiplicity and sameness over difference. Both sameness and unity tend to overlook internal struggles and challenges – the dissonant voices. How about considering 'many-one-ness' where distinctions do not disappear but overlap in messy and complicated ways? Why can't one be both a Jew and in Christ? Why can't I be Indo-Caribbean and in Christ at the same time? Perhaps a more honest (re)reading of Galatians 3:28 may be: 'You are both Jew and Greek, both male and female ... for you are all one in Christ Jesus.' Universality is there but is grounded on cultural and ethnic particularities that live in a dialectic existence (in tension).

We have already noted in our biblical overview the significance of Pentecost in affirming diversity. The miracle of Pentecost consisted not in their making miracle use of the same language but in the fact that, without ceasing each to use their mother tongue, they were, nevertheless, all of them able to understand one another. Barriers were broken down, multiplicity remained while one in Christ. No wonder Irenaeus of Lyons developed an understanding of God as one and many, of creation as reflecting this one-ness and many-ness of God, and of the work of the Son and the Spirit as bringing the whole of creation to its intended conclusion.

CHAPTER 4

Our relational God –
A theology of embrace

Diversity in the Godhead is evident in its tri-unity. The unity and diversity of both the human race and created reality reflect the unity and diversity of a triune God (both God's 'one-ness' and 'three-ness'). And, we see the image of God in God's image bearers (humankind). So Christian God-talk ought not to advance any belief that other human beings are fundamentally different from 'us', somehow lesser made in God's image than 'we' are. Yet, how we deal with identity and difference and with one and many remain a challenge.

In sharing in one baptism in Christ, Christians though different share a common identity in Christ. Differences are embraced, not removed. Miroslav Volf[27] invites us to consider embrace as a relational practice and thereby giving content

[27] Miroslav Volf, *Exclusion and Embrace: A Theological Exploration of Identity, Otherness and Reconciliation* (Nashville: Abingdon Press, 1996), p.20.

to identity (ethnic for instance). As in the trinity, we should see ourselves (our identity) in terms of our relationship with each other. If human beings understand themselves as fundamentally made to image the triune life of embrace, then embrace will be both the mode of pursuing positive identities as well as shape the content of our identities. Exclusion happens when we are unwilling to be inconvenienced or move from our ethno-cultural practices. A way to embrace the identity of self while also understanding that identity is to be connected to the other.

God as creator, redeemer and sustainer, while three distinct persons and roles, exist in relationship. One cannot exist independent of the other nor is there a hierarchy of persons and roles. There is harmony in the diversity. This is the pattern to which we are hardwired for community. Can the trinity open up ways for us to consider the blessings of our diverse life together? Trinitarian faith affirms two things, both the oneness and the many-ness of God, both God's unity and diversity. While each person of the trinity embodies the fullness of divinity, each is distinguished by their individuality. Some theologians and church traditions speak of our trinitarian life as a great dance (a *perichoretic dance)*: a dynamic embrace of generously giving and taking (and coming and going) where all are equal and different but where each defers to the other (I call this 'mutual inconveniencing') because of the love of the great dance! A theology of ethnicity is an invitation to come join such a dance and risk being 'mutually inconvenienced', all made possible by God's demonstration of perichoretic love.

Some implications for our life together

This book is a written resource to help churches to become better at making diversity and inclusion a habit and way of life. It is an invitation to become what we are: an intercultural and inclusive community where we are all in need in our calling to deepen our understandings and experiences of God and of one another. Besides being a gospel imperative, it is also a call to live and act justly. Put another way, in the radical embrace of Christ the pain of injustice experienced by any member of the body diminishes and undermines the health and well-being of the whole body. To draw on Pauline imagery, when one part of the body suffers, is hurt, or is injured the whole body is affected. God-talk around ethnicity is geared to create and nurture spaces where we can sustain our diverse, ethnic and cultural identities (among others) while also affirming those of one another.

Our contention from biblical, theological and

practical realities, is that God's default church must be intercultural, not mono-ethnic/cultural. If there is no diversity, if there are no differences to be embraced, then we must ask questions about whether we are faithfully living into what it means to be church. Becoming an intercultural church is both a vision of what we hope to become, and the process of our faithful response to the call by our God of many-one-ness to share in a common life together. Such a view of our ecclesial life will have implications for our faith and faithfulness. Some of these will include:

1. Reconsidering our understanding of God, how God works in the world, who is Jesus Christ for us today, how we understand scriptures, interrogate inherited traditions and reflect on issues of diversity, church and community. We need to re-engage our 'tradition(s)'. Our God-talk on ethnicity, for instance, must reckon with 'tradition', especially in diasporan and multicultural contexts. At the heart of our God-talk is that of our received traditions, that which is handed over or 'traditioned'.[28] This is important given the dynamic nature of ethnic constructions and ways in which ethnic cross-

[28] See, Mark Griffin and Theron Walker, *Living on the Borders: What the Church can Learn from Ethnic Immigrant Cultures* (Grand Rapids: Brazos Press, 2004), pp.64-76.

overs puncture purist tendencies. Failure to grapple with this will impoverish theological conversations on ethnicity and how cultures and identities 'are dynamic and affected by the ambiguities that emerge as a result of the blurring and confusion of boundaries'[29] caused by multiple factors. It is also important as a tool to help contextualise or 'root' faith and faithfulness In this regard scholars such as Jonathan Tan (an Asian-American) make a case for traditioning. Responding to 'tradition-maintenance' which is more static and can be described as traditionalism, Tan suggests that 'traditioning' which is more dynamic, better reflects the reality that ethnicity (like traditions) evolves on a new and changing landscape. Traditioning gives agency to our mixed or hybridised reality (as a result of the interaction or exchange) facilitating new and evolving meanings. In effect, traditioning remixes, contests, challenges, and re-envisions our theological underpinnings in new and exciting ways. What this means, for instance, is a need to revisit our theology of creation, diversity and anthropology, among others.

---

[29] Jonathan Tan, 'Asian American Catholics and Contemporary Liturgical Migrations: From Tradition-Maintenance to Traditioning' in *Liturgy in Migration: From Upper Room to Cyber Space* by Teresa Berger (Minnesota, Liturgical Press), p.248.

2. Risking transformation grounded on justice, equity and the redress of power. Former things will certainly have to give way so that the new can come to life. It will mean – de-learning and re-learning. A theology of ethnicity has to take conversion seriously as it involves (within the diversity around) a conversion of one's monocentric worldview into a community oriented one. It would mean nurturing the habit of listening to each other's stories with compassion, genuine interest, and entering into the experience of the other. It is a conversion towards a perichoretic[30] weaving of multiple voices. A theology of ethnicity gives agency to a roundtable habit or imagery where all are located equally on the edges or margins – there is no periphery and centre nor insider or

---

[30] *Perichoresis* is a Greek term used to describe the triune relationship between each person of the Godhead. It can be defined as co-indwelling, co-inhering, and mutual inter-relating – which allows the distinctiveness of each to thrive while underscoring that each share in (or is integral to) the life of the other. An image often used to express this idea is that of a 'community of being,' in which each person, while maintaining its distinctive identity belongs to the other and shares the identity of the others (and vice versa). In trying to find words to describe the trinity, theologians of the early church described the *perichoresis* as the dance of love. The relationships between the three Persons of the trinity—'dynamic, interactive, loving, serving'—form the model for our human dance steps.

outsider. The centre and margin is both Jesus at the same time who has come to embrace all and offer abundant life for all

3. Reclaiming the church for what it is – a gift of the Holy Spirit and from God – not a historic/human invention. God's kingdom has come and is coming. We cannot continue to hide behind a community of separation. For God values our ethnicity, our identity, our heritage–and so can we. While ethnic identity cannot wholly define us, nor can it save us, those who walk the way of God in Christ must model what it means to live in unity amid diversity. This becomes our habit not because it is politically correct or because it is the latest theological fad or even because it is a good or pragmatic ideal. We should do so because it is integral to both God's creative and redemptive economy.

4. Honestly wrestling the issue of who holds power in the congregation is certain to come up and creating an environment in which decision-making is shared among all those at the table. We must live out a community of radical engagement. We are well aware that in the midst of our brokenness in a fallen world, we need God's grace and healing if we are going to

embrace unity in diversity as a kingdom value. As believers in Jesus Christ, we need to first seek our healing within our community of faith. We need to promote and engage in intercultural, interpersonal relationships based on love, respect, and equality. We can no longer be diverse for diversity's sake. We must move beyond good intentions about diversity and instead make diversity a habit and way of life in our life together.

5. Recognising difference as a gift to be embraced. The biblical stories we have rehearsed in previous sections have underscored this. We have noted that God's intention is not for uniformity, the erasing of identities or the limiting of diversity and difference. This is important in a context where, as a church, we continue to struggle with issues of race, ethnicity, gender, ability and sexual orientation. We have noted how ethnic diversity (difference) may serve as one way to prevent domination by any one group of people over another. Differences challenge the structures of domination and our own prejudices. In the one Christ, we have been gifted unity, difference and hospitality – all at the same time. Our task is to stop essentialising difference and

93

start building relational hospitality across differences.

Unending thoughts ...

The title that jumped out at us in writing this volume is 'rainbow tapestry'. This is not insignificant. Both metaphors point to interwoven variety. In the case of tapestry, for instance, each thread with its distinctive texture and colour is very important in its contribution to the beauty of the whole. Theologically our very humanity is interwoven. While distinctive and particular, our well-being and wholeness is grounded in our interdependence. The love God intends for us is richest when we are actively engaged in securing the well-being of each other. In learning to participate in 'God's Diversity Dance,' every interaction is going to feel awkward at first. Let not our hearts be troubled! We would not fall offstage from spinning too much, too fast. We have the most patient teacher, who knows what particular challenges each of us faces in body movement, and who demonstrates for us what the dance is supposed to look like. Our dancer-God never tires of explaining the steps again and again. The expansive and generous offer of our dancer-God is enough to lead us out of our fear and comfort zones to come alive in grace space. If you are not already on the dancefloor, why not step out, reach out and join in on God's exciting and surprised-filled perichoretic dance. We can guarantee you an experience of 'never a dull moment'!

Bibliography

John Agard, *Half-Caste and other Poems*, Hodder Children's Books (London, 2005).

Milton Acosta Benítez, 'Ethnicity and the People of God' in *Theologica Xaveriana* 59/168 (2009) 319 [309-330]. [326]

Randall C. Bailey, Tat-siong Benny Liew, Fernando F. Segovia (eds.), *They were all together in one place? Towards Minority Biblical Criticism* (Atlanta: Society for Biblical Literature, 2009).

Roger Ballard, 'Race, ethnicity and culture' in Martin Holborn (ed.), *New Directions in Sociology* (Ormskirk: Causeway, June 2002).

Roger Ballard, 'Negotiating Race and Ethnicity: exploring the implications of the 1991 Census', in *Patterns of Prejudice* (30/3, 1996).

Eric D. Barreto, 'Negotiating Difference: Theology and Ethnicity in the Acts of Apostles', *Slavery & Race* (31/2 Spring 2011).

Gay L. Byron, *Symbolic Blackness and Ethnic Difference in Early Christian Literature* (London and New York: Routledge, 2002).

Stephen Cornell and Douglas Hartmann, *Ethnicity and Race: Making Identities in a Changing World*, 2nd edition (Thousand Oaks, CA: Pine Forge, 2007).

Mark DeYmaz, *Building a Healthy Multi-ethnic Church: Mandate, Commitment and Practice of a Diverse Congregation* (California: Jossey-Bass, John Wiley & Sons, 2007).

Mark DeYmaz and Harry Li, *Ethnic Blends: Mixing Diversity and Your Local Church*, Leadership Network Innovation Series (Zondervan, 2010).

Jione-Havea and Clive Pearson (eds.), *Out of Place: Doing Theology on the Cross-cultural Brink* (London & Oakville: Equinox Press, 2011).

Mark Kreitzer, *The Concept of Ethnicity in the Bible: A Theological Analysis* (Edwin Mellen Press, 2008).

Sheryl A. Kujawa-Holbrook, *A House of Prayer for All Peoples: Congregations Building Multiracial Community* (Virginia: The Alban Institute, 2002).

Mark Griffin and Theron Walker, *Living on the Borders: What the Church Can Learn from Ethnic Immigrant Cultures* (Grand Rapids: Brazos Press, 2004)

Gundry-Volf, Judith, and Miroslav Volf, *A Spacious Heart: Essays on Identity and Belonging* (Harrisburg: Trinity Press International, 1997).

Werner Sollors, 'Introduction: the invention of ethnicity' in *The Invention of Ethnicity* (New York and Oxford: OUP, 1996).

John J. Macionis, *Sociology*, 15th edition (Upper Saddle River, NJ: Prentice Hall, 2010).

W. Eugene March, *God's Tapestry: Reading the Bible in a World of Religious Diversity* (Louisville, Kentucky: Westminster John Knox Press, 2009).

Toni Morrison, *Playing in the Dark: Whiteness and the Literary Imagination*, The William E. Massey Sr. Lectures in the History of American Civilization (New York: Vintage Books/Random, 1993).

Laura Nasrallah and Elisabeth Schüssler (eds.), *Prejudice and Christian Beginnings: Investigating Race, Gender and Ethnicity in Early Christian Studies* (Minneapolis: Fortress Press, 2009).

Bhikhu Parekh, *Rethinking Multiculturalism: Cultural Diversity and Political Theory* (London: Macmillan, 2000).

Clive Pearson (ed.), *Faith in a Hyphen: Cross-cultural Theologies Down Under*, with a sub-version by Jione Havea (Sydney: UTC Publications, 2004).

David Rhoads (ed.), *From Every People and Nation: The Book of Revelation in Intercultural Perspective* (Minneapolis: Fortress Press, 2005).

Letty M. Russell, 'God's welcome in a world of difference' in J. Shannon Clarkson and Kate M. Ott (eds.), *Just Hospitality* (Louisville & Kentucky: Westminster John Knox Press, 2009).

Jonathan Sacks, *The Home we Build Together: Recreating Society* (London & New York: Continuum, 2007).

Atul K. Shah, *Celebrating Diversity: How to Enjoy, Respect and Benefit from Great Coloured Britain* (Suffolk: Kevin Mayhew, 2007).

Sujit Sivasundaram, 'Unity and Diversity: The Church, Race and Ethnicity' in *Cambridge Papers: Towards a Biblical Mind* 17/4 (December 2008), [1–4]

Linbert Spencer, *Building a Multi-Ethnic Church* (London: SPCK, 2007).

David E. Stevens, *A Biblical Theology of Multi-Ethnicity for the Church* (Oregon: Wipf & Stock, 2012).

Wole Soyinka, *Climate of Fear: The Reith Lectures 2004* (London: Profile Books, 2004).

Jonathan Tan, 'Asian American Catholics and Contemporary Liturgical Migrations: From Tradition-Maintenance to Traditioning' in *Liturgy in Migration: From Upper Room to Cyber Space* by Teresa Berger (Liturgical Press: Minnesota).

Miroslav Volf, *Exclusion and Embrace: A Theological Exploration of Identity, Otherness and Reconciliation* (Nashville: Abingdon Press, 1996).

Sze-kar Wan, 'To the Jew First and also to the Greek': Reading Romans as Ethnic Construction' [129-155] in Laura Nasrallah and Elisabeth Schussler Fiorenza (eds.), *Prejudice and Christian Beginnings: Investigating Race, Gender, and Ethnicity in Early Christian Studies* (Minneapolis: Fortress Press, 2009).

PART 3
Resources

MICHAEL JAGESSAR

These resources will help your church consider how some of the issues raised in the book can be taken further. Here you will find group exercises (that could be used alone), and practical suggestions for considering how to become more inclusive with regard to issues around ethnicity.

On building a church that is a 'rainbow tapestry'.

Building on the image of the church as a 'rainbow tapestry' here are some suggestions that will help you to broaden your outreach, help you and your community to grow and create positive responses in a diverse setting.

Take a look at your community

An exercise related to the *Connecting Histories* project – a partnership led by Birmingham City Archives, the Universities of Birmingham and Warwick and the *Black Pasts,* Birmingham Futures group.

Find out what major groups live in the community and learn their history (i.e., length of residence, migration patterns, changes in political, economic, and social status).There are a couple of ways to do this.

- You can start by contacting local government agencies and planning groups. You could also check out the last Census report which is online or the webpage of your local Council; or local community newspapers (often in libraries); drive and walk around the community and pay attention to social activities, housing developments and conditions, street life, etc.; attend community activities and talk to people; and meet with local community leaders.

- Observe and ask about the characteristics that distinguish the groups from one another. Such characteristics could include cultural tradition and ethnicity, socioeconomic class, employment categories, and/or religion.

- Learn about the social organization of the different groups, including their social points, support networks, and major institutions.

- Identify the major events that affect the community. These could include the election of a new mayor who does not value the community's diversity, the closing down of a major factory that cost many residents their jobs, religious insensitivities, far right or extreme groups protest or the expansion of a mental health centre. Consider the links between such events and other changes in the community. Pay special attention to how these events have affected the major groups in the community.

- Identify and attend the events that signify the traditions of the community. Such events could give you insights into whether or not the community values its diversity, what is important to the community, and which group is most visible and valued.

Create an abundant life church

Consider what steps you can take to become the multi-ethnic church that reflects the way of abundant life for all (Jesus' offer):

- Building bridges of love and trust to the people groups of your community. The world is around us. Reach out and build relationships, offer space for people; gather them in ethno-cultural fellowships, and welcome them into the family as one diverse church.
- Welcoming all, allowing space and opportunities for cultural habits and markers to thrive without being separated from the rest of the body of Christ. This helps to re-build social capital for displaced and migrating groups and becomes increasingly important in the second and third generations.
- Considering intentional opportunities for those with a different ethnic background to become part of your church community by gaining practical experience and training in order to access leadership roles.
- Intentionally reaching out in spite of the

cost: This is a long-haul endeavour so be committed to persevere. Becoming a multi-ethnic and intercultural church will require adjustment, compromises and mutual inconveniencing.

Remember: you are not alone.

God, who speaks many languages, is multi-ethnic, embracing diversity with open arms. So invest in inclusive worship; diverse leadership; focusing on a larger goal (God's offer of abundant life in Christ for all); being intentional; investing in developing intercultural competencies; and be open and adaptable to the movement of God's Spirit

Bible based group exercise

James 2: 1-17 Do our words and actions include or exclude?

Martin Luther may have missed the point of James's letter when he referred to it as an 'epistle of straw'. The bottom line for James is that we are all accountable to God for our words and deeds. What do our words and actions say of God's love, grace and generosity? Is the faith that influences our actions modelled after the way of God in Christ?

The author of James is concerned about an understanding of faith that distorts and restricts faithfulness. Faith becomes dead when reduced to a series of statements that Christians profess to believe. Faith is inseparable from faithfulness.

Starting with a query about what faith actually is, James uses the social class of the time as the key issue to explore the question. He exposes the prevailing human tendency to defer to those who are visibly wealthy while dismissing those at the lower end of social standing. Wealth and influence are used as markers with the implications that those for whom these are favourably stacked expect to be the insiders and to receive certain privileges.

By uncovering the excluding pattern of classism and related acts of snobbery, prejudice and favouritism, James's challenge went beyond the 'logic' that the wealthy person is good and the poor person is bad. Pointing back to the central teaching of faith as demonstrated by Jesus: 'Love your neighbour as yourself' (v.8), James puts his listeners (and audience) in an uncomfortable position by underscoring that belief in Jesus must be seen in the practice of the command to love one's neighbour, especially the poor. To ignore the poor is to dishonour God.

In the process, James tackles head-on the problem of discrimination in the Christian community, maintaining that faith in Jesus Christ bears directly upon our treatment of persons. All excluding habits based on social ordering that privileges the rich is a betrayal of the way of Jesus.

It is not insignificant that James speaks of 'acts of favouritism'. By employing the plural he calls to account all forms of prejudice and discrimination based on outward appearances such as disability, ethnicity, class, gender, age, sexuality, dress, etc.

James has much to contribute to our thinking about acts and experiences of discrimination and exclusion. For James discrimination of any kind is inconsistent with Christian faith! And, to work towards justice is a calling Christians cannot pursue by their own strength. We are not alone: it is God's gracious presence and power and wisdom that makes it possible for us to live as James describes.

For reflection

1. Reflect on what your actions suggest about your faith and Jesus' way.

2. James wants the good news to be experienced—by each believer and through each believer to the many others who need a tangible expression of grace. Is it possible that James may be reframing the question: 'Where is the good news for your neighbour?'

3. What has gone wrong in our life together for prejudices and excluding habits, rather than the preferences of God, to be manifested among us?

Web based Resources

The main denominations have resources to help churches in issues related to multi-cultural diversity and awareness.

- Churches Together in Britain and Ireland www.ctbi.org.uk have resources linked with Racial Justice Sunday (usually the second Sunday of September). These resources are helpful for churches exploring issues that are wider than racial justice.
- *Strangers No More* is a training course produced by the Methodist Church. Session One: 'Identity and Roots: Who we are' may be a helpful session to use with your church.
- The United Reformed Church has a series of Good Practice Notes related to multi-cultural ministry. http://www.urc.org.uk/mission/racial-justice-and-multicultural-ministry/good-practice-notes.html
- The Church of England resources are available at www.churchofengland.org – search for 'Minority Ethnic Anglican Concerns'.

Index

110

Index